COUNTRIES  OF THE WORLD

Jack Brickenden

with photographs by Chris Fairclough

Illustrated by Malcolm Walker

Titles in this series

Australia	Italy
Canada	Japan
The Caribbean	The Netherlands
China	New Zealand
France	Pakistan
Great Britain	Spain
Greece	The U.S.A.
India	West Germany

Cover *The Valley of Ten Peaks in the Rocky Mountains, Alberta.*

Opposite *The Canadian National Tower, a Toronto landmark, was built to improve radio and television reception. It is the highest unsupported structure in the world.*

First published in 1988 by
Wayland (Publishers) Ltd
61 Western Road, Hove
East Sussex BN3 1JD, England

© Copyright 1988 Wayland (Publishers) Ltd

3rd impression 1991

Editors: Clare Pumfrey and Philippa Smith
Series design: Malcolm Smythe

British Library Cataloguing in Publication Data
Brickenden, Jack
  Canada.
  1. Canada – For children
  I. Title II. Fairclough, Chris
  III. Walker, Malcolm IV. Series
  971.064'7

ISBN 1-85210-042-7

Typeset by Oliver Dawkins Ltd, Burgess Hill, West Sussex
Printed in Italy by G. Canale and C.S.p.A., Turin
Bound in Belgium by Casterman S.A.

Contents

All words that appear in **bold** in the text are explained in the glossary on page 46.

1 Introducing Canada

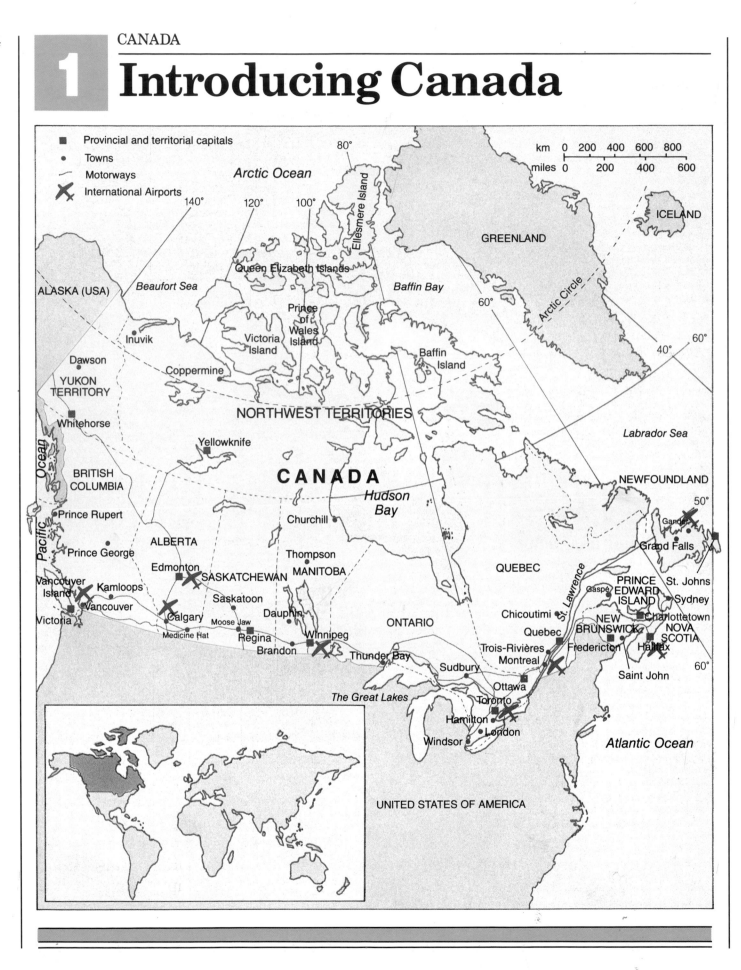

Legend:
- ■ Provincial and territorial capitals
- • Towns
- ⌇ Motorways
- ✕ International Airports

Canada

Land area:	9,970,610 sq km
Population:	26,000,000 (approx)
Capital city:	Ottawa

The Niagara Falls, on the border between Canada and the USA, attract millions of visitors each year. Here, at the famous Horseshoe Falls, the river plunges 55 m.

Canada is the second largest country in the world, yet its population of 26 million is just half that of Britain and one-tenth the population of the USA. Canada is made up of ten **provinces** and two **territories**. The provinces from east to west are Newfoundland, Nova Scotia, Prince Edward Island, New Brunswick, Quebec, Ontario, Manitoba, Saskatchewan, Alberta and British Columbia. The territories are the Yukon Territory and the Northwest Territories.

Canada is perhaps best known as the country where you find **Mounties** in their scarlet uniforms, the famous Horseshoe Falls at Niagara, the tallest building in the world — the CN (Canadian National) Tower in Toronto — and the Calgary Stampede. But there is much more to the story of Canada.

Canada is a land of great variety. There is the frozen **tundra** of the north, the thick forests and high mountains of the Pacific Coast, the vast, flat plains of the prairie provinces, and the forests and lakes of the Canadian Shield. It is also a country with plenty of natural resources. There are areas of rich farmland, productive fishing grounds on both the east and west coasts, oil and gas, and many mineral deposits.

The country is so enormous that it has seven **time zones**. This means that there is a seven hour time difference between the east and west coast. It takes five days and five nights to cross the country by train. But most Canadians live within 160 km of the Canada-USA border, which is the longest undefended border in the world.

Both the French and the British played a vital role in the early development of Canada, and today, French and English are Canada's two official languages. The USA, Canada's powerful and wealthy neighbour to the south, is now the country's most important **ally** and trading partner. The USA has also had a strong influence in shaping Canada's society.

2 Land and climate

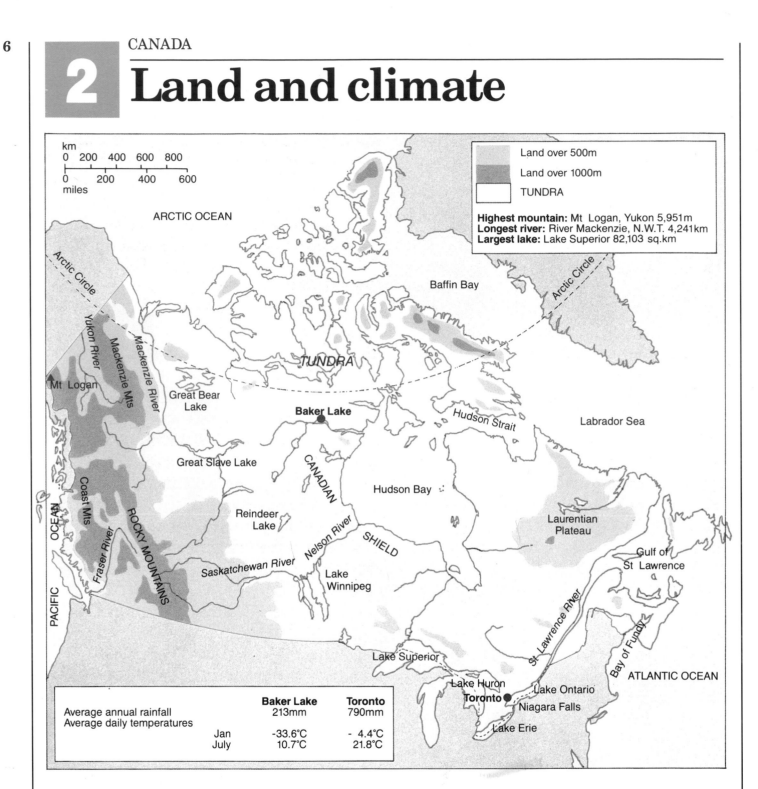

km
0 200 400 600 800

0   200   400   600
miles

ARCTIC OCEAN

Land over 500m
Land over 1000m
TUNDRA

Highest mountain: Mt Logan, Yukon 5,951m
Longest river: River Mackenzie, N.W.T. 4,241km
Largest lake: Lake Superior 82,103 sq.km

Arctic Circle

Baffin Bay

Arctic Circle

Yukon River

Mackenzie Mts

Mackenzie River

Mt Logan

TUNDRA

Great Bear Lake

Baker Lake

Hudson Strait

Labrador Sea

Coast Mts

Great Slave Lake

CANADIAN

ROCKY MOUNTAINS

Fraser River

Reindeer Lake

Hudson Bay

SHIELD

Laurentian Plateau

Saskatchewan River

Nelson River

Lake Winnipeg

Gulf of St Lawrence

PACIFIC OCEAN

Lake Superior

St Lawrence River

Bay of Fundy

ATLANTIC OCEAN

Lake Huron

Toronto

Lake Ontario

Niagara Falls

Lake Erie

	Baker Lake	Toronto
Average annual rainfall	213mm	790mm
Average daily temperatures		
Jan	-33.6°C	- 4.4°C
July	10.7°C	21.8°C

Canada stretches one-fifth of the way around the world and occupies almost the entire northern half of the North American continent. It has an area of nearly 10 million sq km. The country's coastline is more than 250,000 km long, so if you could stretch it out into one long line, like a piece of string, it would wind around the equator six times.

Canada is bounded by the Atlantic Ocean to the east, the Pacific Ocean to the west, the Arctic Ocean to the north, and the USA and the St Lawrence Seaway (sometimes called Canada's fourth sea coast) to the south.

Canada's greatest north-south distance is about 4,500 km, and its greatest east-west distance is about 5,000 km. So some Canadians live thousands of kilometres away from the sea. In its rivers and lakes, Canada contains about one-third of the world's fresh water supply. In fact, Canada has over one million lakes, which is more than the rest of the world combined.

Canadians are used to very cold winters, but in the south they also have very warm summers. The coldest official temperature ever observed in Canada was −63°C in the Yukon in 1947; yet in parts of the country, the temperature also rises to 43°C in mid-summer. This is a range of nearly 106°C. Spring is usually short, and autumn, or Fall, is very colourful and pleasant, especially if there is a warm spell, called an 'Indian summer'.

The huge wilderness area that Canadians refer to as 'the north' stretches towards the North Pole. This includes the tundra, a vast barren plain where it is too cold for trees to grow. It is an ice desert, so called because it is very dry. The little snow that does fall does not melt away. Throughout most of this area, which includes the Yukon and the Northwest Territories, there are only about 60 frost-free days each year.

The snow-capped Rocky Mountains mark the border between British Columbia and Alberta.

The surface of the tundra melts each summer, but the ground below remains frozen all year round. This is called permafrost.

The total population of 'the north' is approximately 70,000. Trapping, hunting and mining are the main activities; farming is impossible. This is called the 'Land of the Midnight Sun', because in the middle of summer the sun goes down for only a few hours a day. In the very far north, it never sets at all for a few weeks every summer.

Right The summer sun melts the sea ice at Cape Dorset, Baffin Island.

Below There are vast areas of forest in British Columbia, where the giant Douglas fir trees grow.

Just south of the tundra is an enormous area of thick forest, rocks, lakes and swamps stretching south-eastwards to the province of Quebec and towards the Atlantic coast. It is known as the Canadian Shield, and it covers half the total land mass of Canada. It is rich in minerals and other natural resources; and towns have grown up around the mines and paper mills.

In the west, the rainforests of British Columbia provide timber that is exported all over the world. The vast grain-growing prairies stretch 1,700 km from west to east and provide one-third of the world's wheat. Central Canada is dairy land and the manufacturing heartland of the country. The Atlantic provinces, including Prince Edward Island, Nova Scotia and New Brunswick, have considerable forestry and mining industries, but a main occupation here is fishing.

Manitoba farmland in early autumn. The wheat-growing prairies stretch across three provinces – Manitoba, Saskatchewan and Alberta.

3 Wildlife

The unsettled areas of Canada, as well as the parks and sanctuaries, are full of wildlife. Wild animals can often be seen by visitors to these areas. There are **moose**, deer, beaver, antelope, bears, mountain lions, mountain sheep, buffalo, lynx, otter and mink. Walrus, seal, sea cows and **narwhal**, along with a multitude of fish, fill the cold Arctic waters. Herds of caribou roam the icy northlands. The timber wolf is often heard, but seldom seen. There is also a great variety of birds, including swans, geese, ducks, eagles and hawks. On a certain day in September, at Hawk Point near Port Stanley, Ontario, thousands of hawks fly south over Lake Erie.

Above The black or cinnamon bear can be found in every province and territory. It is very strong and can be dangerous.

Left The snowy owl is found in the tundra zone.

Several species of bear live in Canada. The great brown bears of north-west Canada are the largest living **carnivores**. Fully grown, they can weigh nearly 700 kg. The famous grizzly bear lives mainly in the mountains of the Canadian west. It is called grizzly because the yellow-tipped long hairs with black roots give its fur a greyish colour. The grizzly, nicknamed 'silvertip', sometimes eats calves, ponies and deer. It is a favourite target for big game hunters.

The mighty polar bears live in the far north. These large greyish-white bears are also fierce **predators**. They live mostly in the water and on ice floes, and eat fish, seals, wolves and birds. Sometimes polar bears wander into populated areas, such as Fort Churchill on the shores of Hudson Bay, in search of food. They have been known to attack humans.

The Canadian black bears are found in wooded areas all across the country. They are **omnivorous**, and eat berries, fish, nuts, frogs, roots, snakes and honey, and sometimes, when times are hard, even small pigs and sheep. The black bear is so strong that all the other animals in the woods stay out of its way.

Today most wildlife is protected by law, but there are brief annual hunting seasons. In the huge **reserves** all over the country the animals are safe from hunters throughout the year. Herds of buffalo, which once ranged the prairies, are now protected in national parks.

Left In the cities there is plenty of wildlife. This raccoon hunts for food in dustbins and gardens.

Below Two bull moose lock antlers in a battle over territory.

4 Canada's history

The first inhabitants of Canada came from Asia about 30,000 years ago, across the Bering Strait to Alaska. Some were **nomads** and others led more settled lives. They were the ancestors of today's **Inuit**.

The Vikings were the first Europeans to arrive. In about AD 1000 Lief Ericson (Lief the Lucky) landed on the Labrador coast. But the Vikings did not stay in the New World for long. In 1497 John Cabot discovered Canada's east coast (now called Newfoundland) and claimed the

Above In May 1497, John and Sebastian Cabot set sail from Bristol in search of China. Fifty-two days later they reached a land they named Newfoundland.

Below In 1534 Jacques Cartier, a French explorer, landed at the Gaspé Peninsular and claimed Canada for France.

A Settler's Log House *painted by Cornelius Krieghoff, a Dutchman who settled in Canada.*

land for Britain. Settlements were founded so that the rich Newfoundland waters could be fished. Both the French and English set up permanent settlements in the new land, and traded with the Canadian **Indians** — furs for guns, liquor and tools. Fur, especially beaver fur to make the tall hats that were in fashion at that time, was in great demand in Europe. Soon shiploads of **pelts** were being sent to Europe.

In 1670, England's King Charles II granted the Hudson's Bay Company the right to trap animals over an area of land whose waters drained into Hudson Bay. This area was half the size of Europe. The fur traders explored the country as they trapped for pelts to sell to the European fur hat market. The fur traders were followed by settlers, and slowly the country was opened up to the Europeans.

While the British were developing the Atlantic area and the central part of the country (Ontario), the French were establishing their own fur-trading operations and settlements mainly in what is now the province of Quebec.

Above In 1759, General Wolfe died at the Battle of the Plains of Abraham, having led the British to victory.

The rivalry between Britain and France led to wars. In 1759 at the Battle of the Plains of Abraham, just outside Quebec City, the British defeated the French. The French territories of the New World came under British control. It was decided that both English and French should be the official languages of Canada, and this has remained the case ever since.

Right Dr Barnardo's Homes sent more than 20,000 British orphans to Canada between 1867 and 1914. They were either placed with Canadian families or cared for in rural training institutions. Canada became known as 'the land of the second chance'.

Canada was a British **colony** for more than a century. In 1867, the British North America Act created the Dominion of Canada, which consisted of Nova Scotia, New Brunswick, Ontario and Quebec. The rest of the provinces and territories joined the confederation by the turn of the century, except Newfoundland, which joined in 1949. The Head of State is still Queen Elizabeth II, and Canada belongs to the **Commonwealth**.

Left The Loyalist Days Festival celebrates the founding of Saint John in New Brunswick. People dress up to re-enact the landing of the first loyalist settlers.

Important dates

1497	John Cabot arrives at the east coast of North America and claims it for Britain.
1534	Jacques Cartier lands at Gaspé Peninsula and claims it for France.
1603	Samuel de Champlain lands in New France (Quebec). Permanent French settlement established.
1610	Henry Hudson explores Hudson Bay for Britain.
1670	Hudson's Bay Company established.
1743	La Verendrye arrives at the Rocky Mountains, claiming them for France.
1759	Britain defeats France at the Plains of Abraham, outside Quebec City.
1792	Captain George Vancouver charts the Pacific coast of Canada.
1812-14	War with the USA.
1857	Ottawa is chosen capital of Canada.
1867	British North America Act creates Dominion of Canada. John A. Macdonald is elected the first Prime Minister of Canada.
1873	The North West Mounted Police, later to become the Royal Canadian Mounted Police, are established.
1901	First transatlantic wireless signal is received by Marconi at Signal Hill, Newfoundland.
1914-18	First World War. Many Canadian servicemen fight with the Allies in Europe.
1921	Sir Frederick Banting and Dr Charles Best discover insulin.
1939-45	Second World War. In 1939, Canada joins the Allies.
1947	Introduction of Canadian citizenship. (Previously, Canadians could only claim British citizenship.)
1949	Newfoundland becomes Canada's youngest province.
1961	St Lawrence Seaway opened.
1976	Olympic Games held in Montreal.
1982	Canada Act is passed by Parliament in Britain, giving Canada full authority over its constitution.
1988	Winter Olympic Games held in Calgary.

5 The people today

Just over a century ago, 3.7 million people called Canada their home. Today, that total is approaching 26 million. Nearly half of Canada's population is of British origin; just over a quarter is of French origin. But in western Canada, half the population is of neither French nor British origin.

The largest **ethnic** group, after the French and British, are the Germans, followed by the Ukrainians, Italians, and people from the Netherlands, Scandinavia, Poland and many other countries. Since the Second World War over 3 million immigrants have come to Canada. The result is an interesting, multi-cultural society. There are also about 300,000 registered Canadian Indians and about 20,000 Inuit, who live in the far north.

Above This man is a Mohawk Indian. He is a high-steel specialist and works on the construction of bridges and high buildings all over the world.

Left The Caribana Festival is a colourful Caribbean celebration which is held in Toronto every year.

Right Alberta is famous as the home of cowboys and cattle ranchers.

Below Canada is a bilingual country, so signs and labels are printed in both French and English in some parts of the country.

Canadian Indians today have the choice of living on reserves and receiving land which they do not have to pay for, or living alongside the rest of the population. If they choose to integrate, they no longer receive special benefits from the government. Some Indians are working their way successfully into mainstream Canadian society, but most prefer to live in the old traditional ways on the reserves, hunting and fishing.

Canada is a **bilingual** society. Nearly seven out of ten Canadians speak English; two out of ten speak French; the rest speak both these official languages.

Most French-speaking Canadians live in the province of Quebec. But business in North America is conducted mainly in English, and so the French-speakers tend to be at a disadvantage. Despite this, brilliant French Canadian leaders, such as Sir Wilfrid Laurier and Pierre Trudeau, have emerged in politics.

The languages of the original peoples of Canada are called aboriginal languages. Although these people make up a very small part of the total population, many have managed to keep their language and culture alive.

The languages that other settlers have brought to Canada are called heritage languages. Canadians are a mixture of people from all over the world who do not forget their own history and culture. Many Canadians speak the language of their homelands privately, or in special ethnic clubs. One radio station in Toronto broadcasts in 30 languages.

6 | Cities

Above *Toronto's bustling Chinatown runs east-west along Dundas Street.*

Right *Vancouver, Canada's third largest city, stands on the Pacific coast at the mouth of the River Fraser.*

In 1867, when Canada became a self-governing nation, only one-tenth of the population lived in cities. Today, eight out of ten Canadians live in the cities, and by the year 2000 this figure is expected to rise to nine out of ten.

Canada's cities vary greatly in appearance. Quebec City is the only walled city in North America, and has kept many of its historic features. Prairie cities, often with Indian names, have wide streets, many of which have numbers rather than names so that it is easy to find any address. Ottawa, the national capital, is a modern city with office buildings of glass and steel overlooking rivers that are still used to transport enormous log booms downstream to the sawmills.

Montreal is the second largest French-speaking city in the world after Paris, and is famous for its cultural life. Toronto, Canada's largest city, has a space-age city hall and the highest unsupported structure in the world — the CN Tower.

In the pioneering days, settlements were found along natural lines of communication, mainly the rivers and lakes. As the railways expanded, new communities developed along the route of the railway, such as Pile-of-Bones (now Regina), Moose Jaw, Medicine Hat, and Jasper (in the Rocky Mountains).

Major cities like Toronto and Montreal are great commercial centres. They have subways (underground railways) so that people can travel to and from their places of work quickly and easily. There is fast-moving surface transport as well, such as the trolleys in Toronto, buses, taxis and private cars. They all combine to help the cities run smoothly and efficiently.

Besides the sophisticated Canadian cities with their financial institutions, music and arts centres, and their mixture of peoples, there are many smaller places that remain distinctly Canadian. There are the fishing ports with their wooden buildings, the Quebec villages, the picturesque small towns of southern Ontario, and the isolated northern communities.

Above *The magnificent Château Frontenac in old Quebec stands high above the St Lawrence River.*

Below *Horse-drawn caleches pull up in Jacques Cartier Square in Montreal, ready to take tourists sight-seeing.*

7 Home life

Two-thirds of Canadian families live in detached houses; one-third live in flats. Most Canadian homes are centrally heated, with the heating unit in the basement. Houses are usually well-insulated against the extreme cold and the extreme heat of the Canadian climate. Most houses are made of wood, except in major cities. This is because there is plenty of good timber to build with, and wood is also an excellent insulator.

Below Sometimes taking skis to school is part of a child's life during the winter.

Above Children usually have their own bedroom, where they can read and do their homework.

Reading, playing games or watching television are the usual ways of relaxing on winter evenings.

A family home usually has two or three bedrooms, a living room, kitchen, bathrooms, basement and, quite often, a recreation or family room. Homes are heated by natural gas, oil, or electricity. Some Canadian families have a swimming pool in their back garden.

A typical day for a Canadian child during the school year starts at about 7.30 am. Breakfast usually includes orange juice, cereal with milk and sugar, toast and jam or honey, and a glass of milk. Most children take a packed lunch to school. School starts at 9.00 am and, in the cities, is usually within walking distance. In the country, most children are picked up by a school bus.

School ends at 3.30 pm for most children, and then it is time for after-school activities such as hockey practice, piano lessons, or else it is play time. In the warm weather this usually means baseball, football, cycling, roller-skating or swimming. In the cold winter weather, children enjoy ice hockey, skating, tobogganing or building snow forts. But there is not so much daylight in winter, so after 5.00 pm play is usually indoors.

Evening is family time. The evening meal is, for most families, a time to come together and share the news of the day. Older children do their homework after they have eaten.

Television is especially popular in winter. Most Canadians live in areas that pick up American TV broadcasts, so many of the programmes they watch are American. There are also plenty of Canadian programmes that children enjoy, although many parents place a time limit on the amount of television their children are allowed to watch every day.

The household menu generally reflects the family's ethnic background, but there are regional specialities as well. The Atlantic provinces enjoy plenty of seafood dishes; and New Brunswick has an interesting vegetable called 'fiddleheads'. The traditional foods of Quebec include *tourtiere*, a rich pork pie, and a delicious pea soup.

At supper time the family come together and share their news of the day.

Maple syrup, either on its own, poured over pancakes and waffles, or when used to make candy (sweets), is a treat for most Canadians. It is made by boiling down the sweet sap of the sugar maple tree, which grows in eastern Canada.

Generally, all Canadian children like the popular foods — hot dogs, hamburgers, ice-cream. The ethnic foods that are available in shops and restaurants throughout the country are more popular with adults.

Above A Canadian Asian family enjoy a summer's day outing to the beautiful Butchart Gardens in Victoria on Vancouver Island, British Columbia.

Left Inuit families live in camps throughout the northern Arctic regions of Canada. This family live on Baffin Island.

8 Education

Public schools are co-educational and free. This junior high school takes children aged from 12-14.

Each province manages its own schools, so the education system varies from province to province. There are several types of school. A 'public school' is one that is financed by taxes and is available to everyone, free. Canadians call a school that charges fees a 'private school'. Within the public school system, some provinces have 'separate schools', which are run by Roman Catholics.

Children start elementary school when they are six. In most provinces elementary school goes to grade six (age 12). Then there are two years of junior high school (to age 14), and finally, high school from grades nine to twelve (ages 15-18). Children must attend school until they are sixteen years old. After high school, students can go to a university or to a community college to continue their studies.

The school year begins early in September and continues until the end of June. Children who go to a public school have a two-month holiday in the summer (July/August), a Christmas break, a mid-winter break of ten days in March, and various public holidays as well, depending on the province.

University students go to classes from mid-September to late April and, in most cases, have nearly five months holiday, during which they take part-time jobs to earn the money to pay for their tuition for the next year. The tourist industry, which is at its busiest in summer, employs many students during the long summer break.

In the pioneering days, and even until twenty years ago, country schools were one-room buildings where one teacher taught all ages, and all the students worked in the same schoolroom. This has all changed. Now, these 'little red schoolhouses' have been bought by city people who have converted them into holiday homes.

Today, country children are picked up and taken by big yellow school buses to a country school, which is just as big and modern and well equipped as any city school. In the far north, children usually attend a 'live-in' school for most of the year. These northern schools serve large areas, so the children have to live at school because they cannot travel 1,500 km to school each morning in a big yellow bus.

Above *Many children are taken to school in big yellow buses like this.*

Left *Art is an important part of the curriculum at high school.*

9 Shopping

In the early days, settlers 'shopped' by trade or barter. This meant they might offer to swop a freshly killed deer or a bearskin for grain or a blanket. This worked well in the wilderness, but in the towns and villages people needed money to buy their goods. The first paper money was introduced into the colony 300 years ago by French soldiers. They used playing cards for money. Because most people could neither read nor write, the playing card system worked well for a while. When the supply ships docked in the New World the colonists cashed in their cards for coins.

In 1817 Canada's first bank notes were printed, and in 1858 the first official Canadian coins were issued. The dollar ($) is Canada's official currency. In North America a dollar is sometimes called a 'buck' — this name comes from buckskins that were traded between Indians and Europeans. The Canadian dollar is worth 100 cents.

Above The dollar is Canada's official currency. The biggest note is $1,000. The coins are 1c, 5c (called a nickel), 10c (called a dime), 25c (called a quarter, for one quarter of a dollar), 50c and $1.

Left The Eaton Centre indoor shopping mall in Toronto.

Above In Toronto the best-known discount store is Honest Ed's, run by Ed Mirvish.

The story of shopping in Canada is the story of the Hudson's Bay Company. Today the company has big department stores in cities all over Canada, but it continues to run small trading posts or general stores in the outlying communities as well, and has a thriving fur-trading operation.

Nowadays, Canadian shoppers can choose from small, neighbourhood shops or the local shopping centre, which is an open-air complex with department stores, shops and a car park. Indoor shopping malls are also popular, especially as they are comfortably warm, no matter what the weather is like outside.

Nowadays, the Hudson's Bay Company runs both city stores and remote trading posts like this one.

10 Sport and leisure

Canada is a land of lakes and rivers, trees and mountains, where many people enjoy the great outdoors in both winter and summer.

The wilderness is never very far from the city centres. People who work all day in the city can, in a very short time, get away from it all and go fishing on a quiet lake. Many people drive to **cottage country** at the weekends or during their holidays. Some even fly planes that land on wilderness lakes. Many Canadian lakes, especially those close to towns and cities, are dotted with cottages and holiday resorts. The cottages are often well-insulated so they can be used in winter to enjoy cross-country skiing, **snowmobiling** and **snow-shoeing**.

Above In winter people can go ice-skating, even in the heart of the cities.

Above Canoeing is a popular sport in summertime.

Left In summer many families like to spend their weekends in a lakeside cottage.

Summer is the usual holiday time for families. Many families spend their summer holiday at a cottage, either their own or a rented one. Camping is also popular. There are many camping facilities throughout the country, either in private camping sites or in the national and provincial parks. Because of Canada's cold winters, some families go to the southern USA for the March break, or to one of the Caribbean or Pacific Islands for mid-winter warmth and sunshine.

Summer sports include baseball, football, tennis, lacrosse (which is adapted from an Indian game), golf, biking and a great variety of water sports, such as water-skiing, scuba diving, whitewater rafting, canoeing and sailing. Ice hockey, skating and skiing are the most popular winter sports for children. Ice hockey is usually played outdoors on natural ice.

New immigrants have brought new sports to Canada. Soccer is growing increasingly popular, and rugby is also played. But cricket is a sport that is rarely played in Canada.

Above Lacrosse is Canada's national sport. It was originally an Indian game known as 'baggatway', but was renamed by French missionaries.

Right Inuit children playing ice-hockey in the street. It is one of the most popular winter sports throughout Canada.

11 Religion and festivals

Traditionally, Canada's peoples staged their festivals according to the change in seasons. For the Indians, spring, when the sap began to flow in the forest, and autumn, which is harvest time, were the main times for festivals.

For the Inuit, who had neither trees nor seasonal harvests, the significant times of year were when the sun went down for the winter and when it rose again in the spring. They would come together for celebrations, which included games such as one-foot high kick, kneel jump and mouth pull. But as Christianity spread through the north, holidays such as Christmas and Easter became their times for celebrating too.

Above In the Thousand Islands, in the great St Lawrence River, church services are held for summer visitors who come in boats and canoes.

Left Immigrants have introduced many different religions to Canada. This is a Russian Orthodox church.

Religious beliefs	Followers (1981)
Roman Catholic	11,210,385
Protestant	9,914,580
Eastern Orthodox	361,565
Jewish	296,425
Muslim	98,165
Hindu	69,500
Sikh	67,710
Buddhist	51,955

The early settlers in Canada brought their religion with them. The French were mostly Roman Catholics; the British mostly belonged to the Church of England and other Protestant denominations, such as Methodist and Baptist. There have been disagreements and problems among the various religious groups, but Canadians have always been free to worship as they wish.

In recent times, a great variety of religious groups have come to Canada, among them Muslims, Hindus, Sikhs and Buddhists. Many immigrants belong to the established religions but prefer to attend services in their own language. So it is not unusual to see a Roman Catholic or an Anglican church with its times of service written in Chinese.

Christmas and Easter are celebrated by all Christians in Canada. These days are also public holidays for everyone. Christmas is a time when most families relax and have fun together. It is especially exciting for young children, who wait to see what presents Santa Claus will bring on Christmas Eve. At Easter, children wait for the Easter Bunny to bring candy eggs.

St Joseph's Indian church at Kamloops, British Columbia.

Thanksgiving Day, in October, is a public holiday throughout the country. It began with the early settlers who celebrated and gave thanks to God for a good harvest. Hallowe'en is also in October. This is when children dress up in fancy costumes and knock on neighbours' doors, crying 'trick or treat'. They make Jack-o'-lanterns by cutting faces in the skin of hollowed-out pumpkins, then they light them up with a candle inside. The lanterns are put in windows to greet Hallowe'en visitors.

Above Ukrainians who live in Canada celebrate their annual festival in Dauphin, Manitoba.

Left Canadian Indians like to hold their traditional ceremonies in full costume. This Indian chief is a member of the Stoney Tribe.

In summer there are many country fairs; the biggest of them all is the Canadian National Exhibition in Toronto. The Calgary Stampede, Buffalo Days at Regina, and Klondike Days at Edmonton are festive occasions for local people and tourists. In winter there is the famous Quebec Winter Carnival, with its ten days of ice sculpture contests and sports.

There are also ethnic holidays and festivals, such as the annual Ukrainian Festival at Dauphin. Everyone celebrates Canada Day on 1 July. This is Canada's birthday, the day Canada became a self-governing nation. There are big firework displays and parades throughout the country.

At Hallowe'en children hollow out pumpkins and carve faces in the skins. They use them as lanterns.

12 Culture and the arts

The first artists in Canada were, of course, the Indians and Inuit, but their work was not regarded as art outside their own communities. The settlers from Europe had brought with them their own ideas of what was and what was not artistic.

In the early part of this century, a group of Canadian artists began to paint the wilderness of Canada as they saw it. Their paintings showed the harsh realities of the Canadian landscape — rocks and lakes, gnarled pine trees, the **northern lights**, the icebergs. These painters were known as the Group of Seven. It took quite a while for Canadians, who in those days still identified with Europe, to accept that this was true art. Gradually, this interest in the true Canada expanded to consider and include the work of the Indians and Inuit as well, such as Chee Chee, Morrisseau and Wescoupe.

The performing arts in Canada have done well in the last 30 years, attracting art and theatre critics from all over the world. Canadian artists no longer have to go to Europe or the USA to gain fame.

Above A detail from The Pointers *by Tom Thomson, one of Canada's most famous artists and a member of the Group of Seven.*

Right The Alberta Ballet Company, one of Canada's many professional ballet companies, performing Coppelia.*

Above There are still strong links with British culture. Canada has its own Stratford, also on a River Avon, where the annual Shakespearean Festival attracts tens of thousands of visitors each year.

Right Traditional Indian totem poles at the entrance to a museum in Victoria, Vancouver Island.

Music and drama festivals are held every year. There are many professional symphony orchestras, as well as a National Youth Orchestra and three opera companies. Winnipeg, Toronto and Quebec have professional ballet companies of international importance.

But Canada has had to struggle to keep its artistic identity. It could easily be swamped by the influence of the USA. Canada's National Film Board and the Canadian Broadcasting Corporation produce films, TV and radio programmes that provide an alternative to American productions.

13 Farming and industry

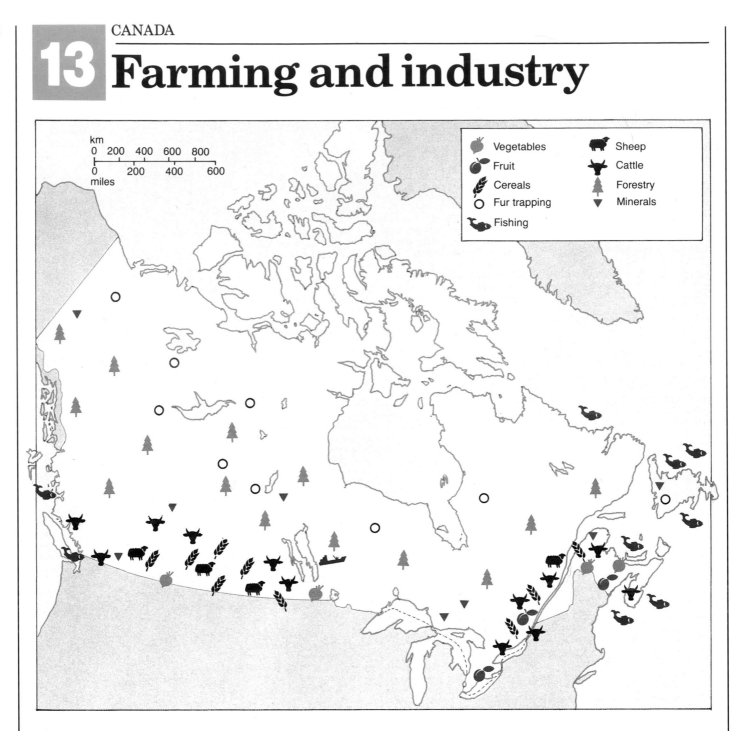

Canada's natural resources appear to be endless. Forests, agriculture, fishing, oil and gas, iron, copper, titanium, asbestos, zinc, uranium, salt, nickel, platinum, gold, potash, silver and furs are all important sources of wealth for Canada.

European adventurers were first attracted to Canada by the abundance of fish in waters off the east coast. Then Canada became the major supplier of furs for the European world. As the country was settled and developed, farming become more important. But much has changed in the last 50 years. At the beginning of the Second World War (1939), Canada, with a population of about 9 million, was essentially an agricultural country. Today, with its population of 26 million, it is primarily a manufacturing country with trading partners throughout the world. Nevertheless, it is still one of the biggest grain-producing countries in the world.

In Canada's Atlantic provinces agriculture, forestry and fishing have always been the main occupations. In New Brunswick, for instance, the early prosperity came from timber and shipbuilding. Today forestry is still important, as well as farming, fishing mining and tourism.

Nova Scotia, a peninsula jutting into the Atlantic Ocean, will always be a fishing province, although oil and gas have been discovered and manufacturing has become important. Prince Edward Island, the smallest of Canada's

provinces, continues to be a farming region. The potato crop and fisheries are its main industries. Newfoundland concentrates on fishing, manufacturing, newsprint (the paper newspapers are printed on) and mining.

In Quebec forestry is the chief industry. Quebec produces over a third of Canada's wood pulp for the papermaking and paper products industries, and three-quarters of the country's large maple sugar and syrup crop. Mining is another important industry (iron, titanium, asbestos, copper and zinc) and there is the production of **hydro-electric power**, a textile industry and tourism.

Main exports:	Forestry-related products, motor vehicles, machinery and equipment, petroleum, wheat.
Main imports:	Motor vehicles, machinery and equipment, electronic equipment, chemicals.

Forestry is British Columbia's first industry. Most of the forest land is government owned.

The prairie provinces are known as the 'breadbasket' of Canada. This is because, in Manitoba, Saskatchewan and Alberta, grain growing is very important. Wheat and other grains are grown across the great plains, which stretch nearly 1,700 km from east to west. Alberta is an important beef producer, too. There is also some mining of nickel, copper, gold and potash, some oil and gas production, and various manufacturing industries.

Left *Fishermen and their catch in the Change Islands, Newfoundland.*

Below *The chimneys of a paper pulp mill in British Columbia pour smoke into the night sky.*

Ontario produces nearly half of Canada's manufactured goods and two-thirds of its manufactured **exports**. The four main manufacturing sectors are transport equipment, food and drink, primary metal and metal fabricating. The Sudbury Basin, nearly 400 km north of Lake Ontario, provides more than one-third of the world's nickel, two-fifths of Canada's copper and it is the western world's largest supplier of platinum.

Ontario uses more electric power than any other province. It is produced one-third by water power, one-third by coal and one-third by nuclear power. Ontario exports one-fifth of Canada's wood products, as well as about one hundred agricultural products, including fruit, vegetables, tobacco, grain, and grapes.

On Canada's Pacific coast, forestry and fishing are big business. Half a million sq km of forest cover more than half of the land in British Columbia. The fishing industry is the most productive of any Canadian province. The salmon is the most valuable catch. Because of its fast-flowing rivers, most of British Columbia's electricity is produced by hydro-electric power stations.

Development of the north — the Yukon and Northwest Territories — began with the Klondike Gold Rush of 1898. Today, most of the gold mines are closed down. Hunting, fishing and trapping are the traditional pursuits, and there is oil and gas production. In some parts of the north, tourism is important. One attraction is the 'longest day' tennis championship on 20 June, when the competition continues far into the night, in broad daylight. The north is estimated to contain nearly half of Canada's mineral resources. It produces zinc, lead, gold, silver and all the country's tungsten.

Above In early spring the maple trees are tapped for their sugary sap. This is called 'sugaring off' and is a great tourist attraction. The fresh maple syrup is sold to visitors.

Below Workers on one of the great prairie farms of Saskatchewan.

14 Transport

The first highways were the rivers and lakes and the birch-bark canoe was the best type of transport. Indians, and later, explorers, fur traders and missionaries travelled thousands of kilometres throughout Canada by canoe. In 1885 the Canadian Pacific Railway, which runs from the Atlantic to the Pacific coast, was completed. Later, another trans-Canada railway system, Canadian National Railways, was developed, which also served the isolated communities. The railway is still an important means of transport.

A Canadian Pacific Railway freight train makes its way through the foothills of the Rockies.

Canadian International Airways is one of Canada's airlines. It provides an international service and regular internal flights.

After 1918 small aircraft began to be used all over northern Canada. Early **bush pilots** flew to remote lakes. They landed on the water using floats in summer and skis in winter. They brought supplies and mail to the people of distant communities. They took away with them articles of trade and people in need of medical treatment. The bush pilots still remain the only practical link with civilization for the tiny outposts and villages in the Canadian north. Today, jet planes provide a regular service to the larger northern centres and air travel has become as simple as taking a bus.

The St Lawrence Seaway carries shipping from all over the world. The Seaway is operated jointly by Canada and the USA. It stretches for nearly 4,000 km into the heart of the continent along the St Lawrence River, and through Lakes Ontario, Erie, Huron, Superior and Michigan.

Right Large articulated trucks cover thousands of kilometres on the modern highways that cross Canada.

Below In Porpoise Bay, British Columbia, small taxi float-planes wait at the jetty for passengers.

15 CANADA
Government

Above *Nowadays, the Mounties wear the scarlet uniforms only on ceremonial occasions.*

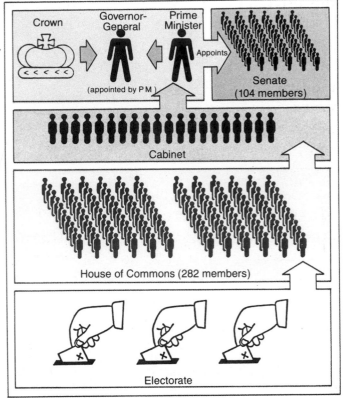

The structure of the Canadian government.

Canada's ten provinces and two territories each have their own **legislature**. The country's political structure is called **federalism**. The division of power between Ottawa (seat of the federal government) and the provinces has changed over the years.

Each Canadian province has its own government and is responsible for internal matters such as roads, housing, policing and education. Each provincial legislature is led by a premier who, like the prime minister in the federal parliament, is the leader of the political party with a majority in the provincial parliament. The main political parties are the Progressive Conservatives, the Liberals, and the New Democratic Party (NDP). At the town and city level the government is in the hands of elected aldermen and councillors.

Canada was the first country to become an independent member of the British Commonwealth, and is now what is known as a **constitutional monarchy**. Queen Elizabeth II is officially Head of State but she does not actually govern or take an active part in the country's political life. The Queen is represented by the Governor-General.

There are three levels of law enforcement in Canada. The national force is called the Royal Canadian Mounted Police (RCMP), or Mounties. There are provincial police forces in Ontario and Quebec, and also city, town and village police. In the eight provinces and two territories where there are no provincial or territorial police, and in the many small, and often very remote, communities with no local police forces, the Mounties are responsible for maintaining law and order.

In the Yukon, where the RCMP handles all three levels of policing, there is a force of 126 members handling an area of 536,326 sq km.

Above Some municipal (town and city) police use bright yellow cars with 'To Serve and Protect' printed on them.

Below The centre of the Canadian government is in the Parliament Buildings in Ottawa, the national capital.

16 Facing the future

At the turn of this century some people were fond of saying that the twentieth century belonged to Canada. History has proved them right. In this century Canada's population has trebled. Canada is no longer a British colony but an independent agricultural and industrial nation. The Canadian standard of living is among the highest in the world. Today, Canadians are placed all over the world as part of a programme to assist **developing countries** under the Canadian International Development Agency (CIDA). In fact, Canada ranks second in the world in giving aid to these countries. Airports in the Caribbean, and radio and television services in some developing countries owe their existence to Canada.

Traditionally, Canada's greatest problem has been the conflict between French and English Canada. However, Quebec's special place in Canada has now been officially recognized, and the old bitterness is gradually fading. New **immigrants** have helped to bridge these old divisions.

Although it was the fur trade that opened Canada to European civilization, in recent years there has been growing pressure, particularly from Europe, to stop the killing of seals for their skins. But Canada's northern peoples have become dependent on fur trading as a way of life and they are concerned that if the fur harvesting is banned, they will lose an important source of livelihood.

Pollution is another major concern for Canada, particularly **acid rain**. There is a growing fear that the acid rain caused by industrial pollution in both Canada and the USA will destroy the lakes and forests of Canada. So far, the Canadians and Americans have been unable to solve the problem. Oil spillages from ships travelling on the Great Lakes and along the coasts of Canada are also a constant threat.

Left Large areas of Canadian forest are slowly being destroyed by acid rain.

Above A harp seal pup. International pressure to stop killing seals for their skins threatens the livelihood of Canada's northern communities.

Canada is not one of the world's great powers, partly because its population is small, and partly because it is a young country that has no tradition of international politics. Canada has two very powerful neighbours — the USA to the south, and the USSR across the Pole to the north. It is too large to defend in the event of world conflict. However, Canada is a young and vigorous country, and home to millions of immigrants from all over the world. It is a land of vast resources and great potential. Canada has been able to find peaceful, workable solutions to its problems in the past, and will no doubt continue to do so in the future.

EXPO 86, the world's fair, was held in Vancouver. The theme was 'World in Motion — World in Touch'.

Glossary

Acid rain Rainwater polluted by waste gases in the air, which upset the chemical balance of the water and can cause harm to plants and animals.

Ally A country, person or group united with another.

Bilingual Speaking two languages equally well.

Bush pilot Someone who flies a light aircraft into remote areas to provide communications, delivery and rescue services where there is no other practical link with the outside world.

Carnivore A creature that feeds on animal flesh.

Colony A land occupied and governed by people from another country.

Commonwealth The association of states that are, or have at some time been, ruled by Britain. There are now 49 independent member states. Queen Elizabeth II is Head of State of 18 of these countries, including Canada.

Constitution The basic political principles by which a state is governed.

Constitutional monarchy Government by a king or queen whose powers are limited by the constitution.

Cottage country The term used by Canadians to describe the wilderness areas used for holiday homes.

Developing countries The poorer, less developed countries of the world, such as most of Africa, Asia, Central and South America.

Ethnic Relating to people who have the same racial, religious or cultural characteristics.

Exports Goods sold to a foreign country.

Federalism A form of government in which power is divided between one central and several regional governments.

Hydro-electric power Power generated by the pressure of falling water.

Immigrants People who come into a country from abroad to settle there permanently.

Indian The name given to the North American aboriginal peoples in error by Christopher Columbus, who thought he had landed in India. There are about 300,000 Canadian Indians. Some of them prefer to be called Native Americans.

Inuit A North American people living traditionally in Arctic regions. They are often referred to as Eskimos, meaning 'flesh-eaters', but this is a name they do not like. About 20,000 Inuit are known to live in Canada.

Insulator A material which does not conduct heat well.

Legislature A group of people appointed to make laws.

Maple syrup Syrup made from the sap of the hard maple tree, commonly referred to as the sugar maple. It takes about 180 litres of sap to produce 4.5 litres of syrup.

Moose A kind of elk or deer found in North America. It is the largest member of the deer family.

Mounties The popular nickname given to the Royal Canadian Mounted Police.

Narwhal A kind of whale, with a single spiral tusk.

Nomads People who travel from one place to another in search of pasture and food.

Northern lights Coloured lights seen in the sky in northern countries in winter. The lights are produced by electricity high in the atmosphere. Astronomers call them aurora borealis, meaning northern dawn.

Omnivorous To feed on both plants and animals.

Pelt The skin of a furry animal.

Predator An animal that hunts and kills other animals for food.

Province A district or region which is governed as a unit of the nation.

Reserves Areas of government land reserved for the use of an Indian tribe, or for the preservation of forests or wildlife.

Snowmobiling Travelling on a sled-like vehicle which has skis at the front and wide caterpillar tracks for drive. It was invented by a 15-year-old Canadian boy, Armand Bombardier.

Snow-shoeing Snow shoes are usually made from rigid webbing on a wooden frame. A snow shoe is attached to each foot to permit walking on deep snow that would not otherwise support human weight.

Territory A region having a certain amount of self-government but not having the status of a province. The Yukon and Northwest Territories are the two Canadian territories.

Time zones The 24 sectors into which the world is divided, by international agreement, for convenience in calculating standard time. Each sector represents 15° of longitude, which is a time interval of one hour. Canada has seven time zones.

Tundra A frozen treeless Arctic region.

Whitewater rafting A sport in which groups of people travel down a river and over rapids in a large rubber raft.

Books to read

Alexander, Brian and Cherry *Eskimo Boy* (A & C Black, 1979)

Brickenden, Jack *We Live in Canada* (Wayland, 1984)

Bryant, Adam *Canada – Good Neighbour to the World* (Dillon Press, 1987)

Cary, Pam *North American Food and Drink* (Wayland, 1988)

Harrington, Lyn *Let's Visit Canada* (Burke, 1981)

Harris, Jeanette *Canada, the Land and its People* (Macdonald, 1982)

Lambert, David *Polar Regions* (Wayland, 1987)

McCullagh, Sheila *The Canadian Arctic – on the edge of the Frozen Sea* (Longman, 1980)

Moon, Bernice and Cliff *Canada is my Country* (Wayland 1985)

Smith J.H.G. *Eskimos – The Inuit of the Arctic* (Wayland, 1984)

Winks, H.L. and R.W. *The St. Lawrence* (Wayland, 1980)

Picture acknowledgements

All photographs are from the Chris Fairclough Colour Library with the exception of the following: B & C Alexander 23 (bottom), 27 (bottom), 29 (bottom), 45 (top); Jack Brickenden 16 (top), 27 (top), 28 (bottom left and right); Canada House, London 14 (bottom), 15, 16 (bottom), 32 (top), 34 (both), 38 (top), 39 (top); Canadian International Airlines 40 (top); Bruce Coleman Ltd 32 (bottom/Halle Flygare); Michael Dent 19 (top), 23 (top), 39 (bottom); Cefyn & Sandra Gauden 25 (bottom); Government of Canada 10 (top); Jonathan Grant 10 (bottom), 11 (both); Jim King 30 (top); Peter Newark's Western Americana 12 (both), 13, 14 (top); Stratford Festival, Canada 35 (top); ZEFA 5, 8 (top), 9, 19 (bottom), 29 (top), 33, 42 (bottom), 43 (bottom). The maps and diagrams on pages 4, 6, 36 and 42 are by Malcolm Walker.

Index